Experimenting with MAGNETS

NAGH

CHO. CHILL CHAINNIG
ny County Library

EN'T RTMENT

WITHDRAWN

D1337670

Nicolas Brasch

Nelson Thorne

KILKENNY COUNTY LIBRARY

KK353299

Nelson Thornes

First published in 2007 by Cengage Learning Australia
www.cengage.com.au

This edition published in 2008 under the imprint of Nelson Thornes Ltd,
Delta Place, 27 Bath Road, Cheltenham, United Kingdom, GL53 7TH

10 9 8 7 6 5 4 3 2
11 10 09 08

Text © 2007 Cengage Learning Australia Pty Ltd ABN 14058280149
(incorporated in Victoria)

The right of Nicolas Brasch to be identified as author of this work has been asserted by him/her
in accordance with the Copyright, Designs and Patents Act 1988

All rights reserved. No part of this publication may be reproduced or transmitted in any form or
by any means, electronic or mechanical, including photocopy, recording or any information storage
and retrieval system, without permission in writing from the publisher or under licence from the
Copyright Licensing Agency Limited, of 90 Tottenham Court Road, London W1T 4LP.

Any person who commits any unauthorised act in relation to this publication may be
liable to criminal prosecution and civil claims for damages.

Experimenting with Magnets
ISBN 978-1-4085-0148-1

Text by Nicolas Brasch
Edited by Johanna Rohan
Designed by James Lowe
Series Design by James Lowe
Production Controller Seona Galbally
Photo Research by Michelle Cottrill
Audio recordings by Juliet Hill, Picture Start
Spoken by Matthew King and Abbe Holmes
Printed in China by 1010 Printing International Ltd

Website www.nelsonthornes.com

Acknowledgements
The author and publisher would like to acknowledge permission to reproduce material from
the following sources:
Photographs by Photographs by AGEFotostock/ S.T. Yiap, p. 9 top; Digital Stock, p. 12 bottom; Istockphoto, p. 12 top/ John
Kraft, p. 4 left/ Jose Antonio Santiso Fernandez, p. 10/ Wiebe Wagemans, p. 5 right; Lindsay Edwards, front and back cover,
pp. 1, 3, 8, 16-23; Masterfile/ David Muir, p. 13; PhotoEdit Inc/ Spencer Grant, p. 9 bottom; Photolibrary/ Ace Photo Agency,
p. 4 right/ Alex Bartel, p. 14/ Cordelia Molloy, p. 15/ Photo Researchers, pp. 6 bottom left, 6 right/ Sinclair Stammers, p. 7/
SPL/ Ben Johnson, p. 6 top left/ Superstock, p. 11/ Terry Sheila, p. 5 left.

Kilkenny County
Library
Acc No KK 353299
Cl. No JMM
Inv No IN 87676
CARLOW EDUC
17/12/08

Experimenting with MAGNETS

Nicolas Brasch

KILKENNY COUNTY LIBRARY

Contents

Chapter 1

MAGNETS

Magnets are objects that are able to draw some other objects towards them.

Some magnets are formed naturally, like rocks that small metal objects can become attached to.

Other magnets are man-made, like the magnets used to attach things to the fridge.

5

All magnets have two things in common.

First, they contain **magnetised** metals like iron, cobalt or nickel.

iron

cobalt

nickel

this rock has iron in it

Iron, cobalt and nickel are metals that have magnetic qualities.
A rock that attracts metal objects will have magnetised metals in it.

Second, all magnets have two poles.
One pole is called the north pole.
The other pole is called the south pole.

When two magnets are put together, unlike poles **attract** each other and like poles **repel** each other.

The north pole of one magnet will attract the south pole of another magnet.

But two north poles, or two south poles, when put together, will repel each other.

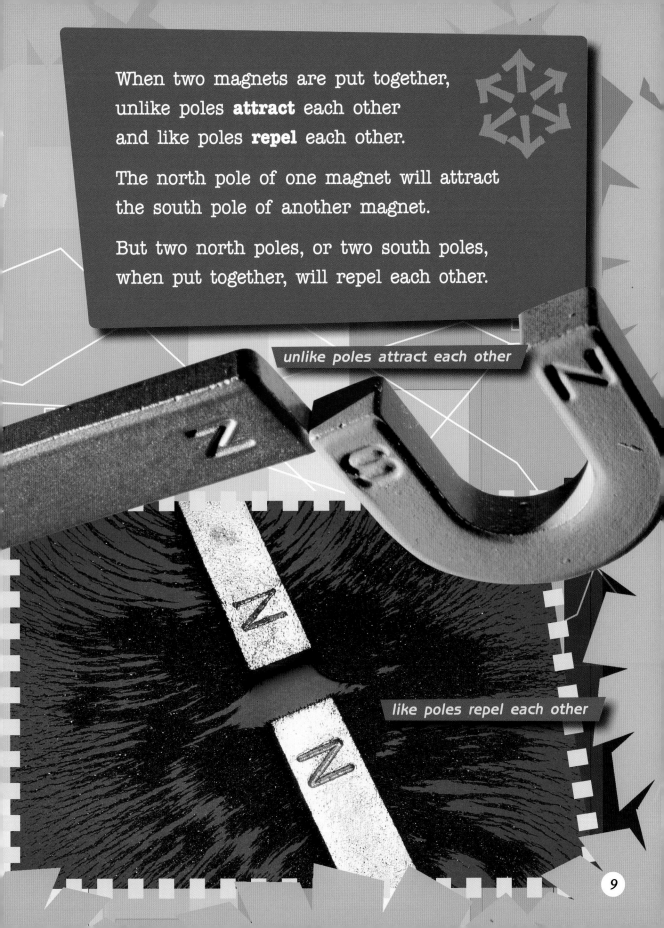

unlike poles attract each other

like poles repel each other

THE COMPASS

One of the most important inventions in history uses a magnet.

This invention is the compass.

Running Words 164

a compass

People have been using compasses
for more than 1000 years.

A compass helps people to work out where they are.

KK353299

The Earth acts like a giant magnet.
It has two magnetic poles called
the north magnetic pole and the south magnetic pole.

The main part of a compass
is a needle that has been magnetised.
The needle is attracted to
the Earth's north magnetic pole.

When someone turns the compass,
the needle will always turn and point
to the Earth's north magnetic pole.
Knowing the direction of magnetic north
can help people find their way when they travel.

Chapter 3

ELECTROMAGNETS

Another important invention combines magnets with electricity, to create electromagnets.

An electromagnet is a special magnet that works when an **electric current** flows through it.

When the electric current is turned off, the electromagnet stops working like a magnet.

This type of magnet is used for picking up
heavy metal objects like scrap metal.

When the electric current flows through the electromagnet
the electromagnet picks up the scrap metal.
When the electric current is turned off,
the scrap metal is dropped.

Chapter 4

EXPERIMENT 1

Aim

To turn an ordinary nail into a magnet.

Materials

- 1 magnet
- 1 iron nail
- some paper clips

Procedure

1. Stroke the nail about 50 times with the end of the magnet. Always use the same end of the magnet and always stroke in the same direction.

2. Pick up the paper clips with the nail.

Observation

The nail picks up the paper clips.

Conclusion

The nail has been magnetised
and acts as a magnet.

Chapter 5

EXPERIMENT 2

A magnetic field is the area around a magnet in which the magnet can affect other objects.

Aim

To observe the effect of the magnetic field around a magnet.

Materials

- magnets of different shapes and sizes
- an acetate sheet
- some iron filings

Procedure

1. Place a magnet under the acetate sheet.
2. Sprinkle the iron filings onto the acetate.

Observation

The iron filings form a pattern.
Using different shaped magnets causes
different patterns to form.
Most iron filings
move near the magnet's poles.

Conclusion

The iron filings show
that magnets produce a magnetic field.
The magnetic field is the strongest
at the magnet's poles.

EXPERIMENT 3

You will need adult supervision.

Aim

To make an electromagnet.

Materials

- 1 piece of plastic-coated copper wire, about 1 metre long
- wire strippers
- 1 large iron nail
- 1 9-volt battery
- some pins or paper clips

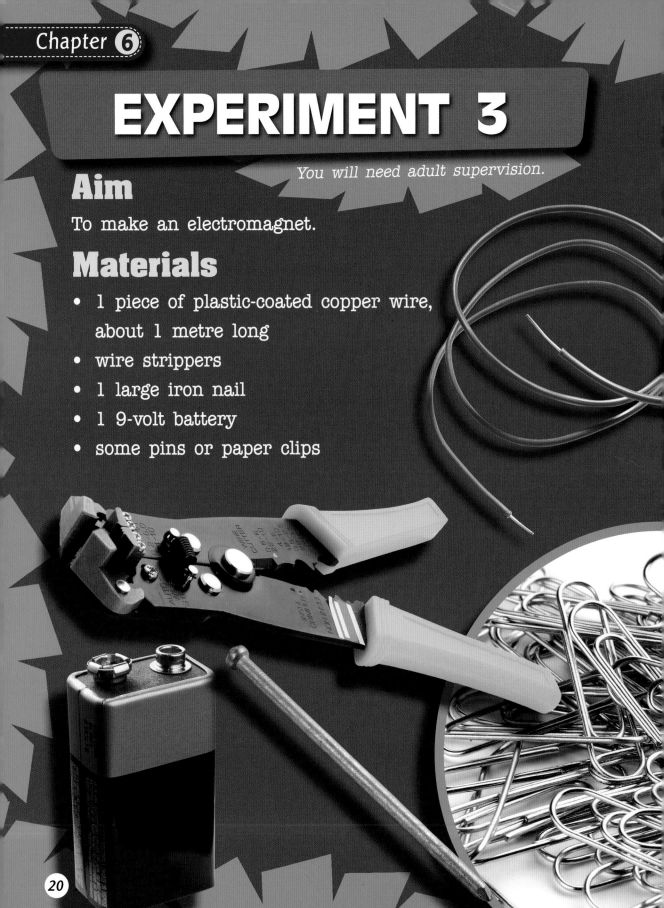

Procedure

1. Cut about 2 centimetres of plastic from each end of the wire using the wire strippers.
2. Tightly wind the wire around the nail.
3. Leave enough wire at each end to twist together.
4. Connect one end of the wire to one battery terminal. Connect the other end of the wire to the other battery terminal.
5. Pick up the paper clips with one end of the nail.
6. Now, remove both ends of the wire from the battery terminals and try to pick up the paper clips.

Observation

When the wires are attached to the battery terminals, the nail picks up the objects.

When the wires are removed
from the battery terminals,
the nail doesn't pick up the objects.

Conclusion

The nail only acts like a magnet
when the electric current
flows through the wire coil.

Glossary

attract   to pull towards

electric current the flow of electric charge

magnetised   something possessing magnetic qualities

repel   to push away

Index